Praise for
What the Dog Said

"I laughed out loud. Went back, re-read the story, and laughed again. I cried. I read the story again, and wiped more tears away. Joanne has shared the best parts of her writing, told from the heart, offered without shame. Man, woman or child, if you're human, this book is for you."

Yvonne DiVita
Founder
BlogPaws Online Pet Community

"A delightfully fun read, filled with wit and a touch of wacky wisdom, Brokaw's anecdotes reveal slices of daily life most of us experience but few of us have the spunk to express."

Lamar Keener
Publisher
Christian Examiner Newspaper Group

"Life happens, and the lessons we learn along the journey determine our destiny. In this life-affirming collection of essays and articles, Joanne candidly reveals the wisdom gleaned and lessons learned that have set her on a path to joy and success. Through tears and laughter, you'll likely find a reflection of yourself as Joanne wittingly shares her own experiences. Sometimes sad, sometimes joyous, and sometimes just downright quirky, life is a true story...and no one can narrate it quite like Joanne."

John Lanier
Executive Editor
Christian Voice Magazine

"**What the Dog Said** made me cry...twice. Without a doubt the BEST dog story in short form I have ever read. Beautiful and powerful. Able to say with such few words what an entire novel by others could not."

Torry Martin
Actor, Author, Screenwriter & Creator of
Adventures in Odyssey character, Wooten Bassett

"Life is funny and packed with poignant life lessons. So is Joanne Brokaw's **What the Dog Said**. This book reminds us that each day is an adventure filled with yucks of laughter and yucks of boogers (from dogs and kids). Tickle that funny bone; pluck those heart strings; read this book!"

Kelsey Timmerman
Author of
Where Am I Wearing and *Where Am I Eating*

"Joanne's unique ability find humor in the everyday things that life throws our way it intricately woven throughout this book. **What the Dog Said** is witty, insightful and a true pleasure to read. Her dog Bandit provides his own canine perspective on holidays like Valentine's Day, Halloween and Christmas, that will make you smile. The final chapter, from which the book gets its name, was my favorite chapter of all. It will touch the heart of anyone who's ever owned a dog...all I can say is keep the Kleenex handy."

Barbara McSpadden
Co-Publisher
Rochester Woman Magazine

"I actually LOLed reading Joanne's witty, whacky and warm-hearted book. Okay, I didn't ROFL, laugh off body parts, or anything like that, but I did LOL and you will too."

James N. Watkins
Humorist, Columnist & Author of
Writing with Banana Peels

"**What the Dog Said** is as reassuring as a devoted Labrador. Joanne Brokaw's reflections mirror the irony, humor, and uncertainty that make each of us adorable."

Suzette Martinez Standring
Award-winning Author of
The Art Column Writing

"I want to hang out with Bandit, call him when my day is less than stellar, commiserate over bad days, and tail wag with him when times are on the upswing. Bandit and his mommy weave clever tales of short prose—bite-sized nuggets, if you will—in the name of dog. What a refreshing compilation of short stories involving our very best friends. Now to get a play date with Bandit: On my must-do list. This dog's future is on fiyah!"

Carol Bryant
Founder
FidoseofReality.com

WHAT THE DOG SAID

WHAT THE DOG SAID
AND OTHER ADVENTURES IN EVERYDAY LIFE

by

JOANNE BROKAW

WordCrafts

What the Dog Said
Copyright © 2013
Elizabeth Joanne Brokaw

Cover design by Bryan Alexis

All rights reserved. No part of this book may be reproduced, stored in a retrieval system, or transmitted in any form or by any means – electronic, mechanical, photocopy, recording, or otherwise – without the prior written permission of the publisher. The only exception is brief quotations for review purposes.

Published by WordCrafts Press
Tullahoma, TN 37388
www.wordcrafts.net

Contents

Books I Never Wrote, and One I Did 1
12 Ways To Know You're Ready To Get A Puppy 5
Going For Gold In My Sleep 9
Paws, Claws and Deep Dog Breaths 13
Big Lies About Valentine's Day 16
Do You Have A Receipt For That? 19
Beauty Is Soul Deep 22
You've Been Shopped! 25
There Is Life After High School 28
Being Successful At Being 40-Something 32
But I Can Explain 35
Confessions of an Office Supply Addict 40
Treat Your Spouse Like A Dog 43
Insomnia 46
Fit, Green and Squashed 49
Happy Halloween! 52
Mind Reading Mommy 55
Puppy Love Is Messy Business 60
Flying the Friendly (and Expensive) Skies 64
The Insanity of Motherhood 67
The Trouble with Technology 70
Twilight in Dog Years 73
Walking Detail 77
Writing Is a Dangerous Job 80
Smooth Talker 84
The Story of Christmas 87
The Perfect Gift 90
The Unsung Celebrity 93
What the Dog Said 96

For my mom

Introduction
Books I Never Wrote, and One I Did

I feel badly for those poor souls who, upon learning that I'm a writer, ask if I've ever been published and are disappointed when I tell them that yes, I've been published in dozens of magazine and newspapers across the US and Canada, and even in one publication on the other side of the world.

"No book?" they ask hopefully.

"No book," I respond, and they quickly change the subject.

Most people, including writers, fall for the myth that if you haven't published a book you're not a real writer. So over the years, in an effort to bolster my own self-esteem as well as that of my friends and family, I've tried to write a book. It's not as if I don't have several (really great) book ideas in my head. I'm just not so sure anyone wants to read what I have to say.

Here are some of the ideas I've been working on over the last decade:

Answers to Questions You Didn't Know You Needed to Ask

Written with my Aunt Mary Ellen, who, under the influence of a single glass of beer, will give away her secret cache of beauty and life secrets in the interest of bettering humanity. Answers in the book will include:

A: If it floats in water, it's fresh
A: Three weeks and don't scratch the rash
A: NEVER! Most people don't know it can kill you

We're still debating whether to include the questions or hold them back for our next book. Really, what writer doesn't want to sign a publishing deal for a series?

Stupid Is As Stupid Does: An Anthology

I got this idea for a collection of stories after leaving the movie theater one very cold and blustery winter night. I started my car, cranked up the heat, and stepped into the nearly empty parking lot to brush the snow off the windows.

As I heard the door slam behind me, I realized that I'd locked my keys in the car and left the engine running. On the passenger's seat, mocking me from the car's toasty warm interior, was my purse, which contained my cell phone and a spare door key (just in case I ever locked my keys in the car).

Around The World In 80 Bugs

I once went on a mission trip to Mexico to help with construction at a school for deaf children. Considering that I don't speak Spanish, don't know sign language, hate to fly and don't know a hammer from a screwdriver, it was a pretty interesting trip.

I went a week without a hairdryer and endured bugs in my bed (and in the shower, on the tables, on the chairs, crawling on my dinner plate). Weeks later I was still picking concrete out of my hair.

My family and friends found my recap of the adventure so entertaining they thought it would be fun to plop me down in other foreign countries, like Canada or Las Vegas, to see what happens.

It's Nothing a Little Zoloft Can't Fix

Wit, wisdom and encouragement for people who suffer from depression, anxiety and other slight mental imbalances.

This book would include practical advice on how to survive a panic attack, ways to convince the emergency room doctor that, despite what his tests and machines say, you really are dying, tips for choosing the best pajamas to wear during a major depressive hibernation and excuses you can use to avoid leaving the house for at least three months.

I've got more where those came from. I even contemplated writing a book containing only summaries of all the books I never wrote. I figured that at least when people ask if I've ever been published, I'd be able to finally say, "Yes," without embarrassment.

But then I was going through piles of old columns and someone casually said, "You've got enough material here for a book."

What? A book? I've already written a book? Written it piece by piece, essay by essay, column by column, year by year?

Apparently so. And most of it is stuff people actually wanted to read, stuff editors actually paid me to write.

The columns and essays collected here have been printed in dozens of magazines and newspapers across a span of several years. Some of the pieces are funny, some are thoughtful, some are just silly and a few were penned by my dog, Bandit. (That's right. My dog is a writer, too.)

I chose my favorites, the ones that still make me laugh or get a little misty-eyed after all of these years. The only new piece in the collection, "What the Dog Said," ended up being the book's title.

While not everything in this book deals with dogs, everything I've written for almost 15 years has in some way been influenced by incessant barking, dog hair in my tea or paw prints on my keyboard. I am who I am because of dogs - those barking in the room right now and those romping around on God's Farm in the Sky.

So, without further ado, I present **What the Dog Said**. I hope you laugh. You may shed a tear or two. Either way, I hope you enjoy reading these pieces as much as I enjoyed writing them.

1
12 Ways To Know You're Ready To Get A Puppy

A friend told me her husband and son were trying to convince her to get a puppy.

"I'm trying to be positive about the whole thing," she explained as she asked her dog-owning friends for advice.

Being the owner of two incredibly intelligent and well-behaved dogs, I was more than happy to share my own thoughts on how to know if you're ready to get a puppy.

1) Volunteer to pick up the neighbor dog's poop for a week. If at the end of seven days the task seems like a treasure hunt instead of a chore, you might be ready to get a puppy.

2) Pour a measuring cup full of dirt onto your freshly laundered bed sheets. If after sleeping on them for several days you find you enjoy the feeling of crunchy linens because it reminds you of your last vacation at the beach, you might be ready to get a puppy.

3) Have your spouse take one shoe from every pair of shoes you own and hide them somewhere in your home. If you can still get to work on time every day, wearing shoes that match, you might be ready to get a puppy.

4) Get up at 5 a.m. every morning and walk around the block, stopping at every telephone pole, tree and fence post. Stand there repeating the phrase, "Go potty. Please go potty." If patrolling your neighborhood like this, especially in the rain or snow, seems like a good way to start your day, you might be ready to get a puppy.

5) Cash your next two paychecks. Drive to your local veterinary hospital and hand over all the money to the vet. If you don't suffer a massive heart attack on the spot, you might be ready to get a puppy.

6) Several times a day, tip over the kitchen garbage pail. Strew the contents around the living room, dining room and kitchen. Then clean it up. If you are overjoyed at finding banana peels under the sofa cushions, you might be ready to get a puppy.

7) Tie a rope around a 50 lb. block of cement and attempt to drag it around the block. If this seems like a

fun way to tone your biceps, you might be ready go get a puppy.

8) Position two 20 lb. bags of bird seed end to end on your bed so that they mimic a 40 lb. dog stretched diagonally across your mattress. If you can sleep comfortably night after night on the remaining space, you might be ready to get a puppy.

9) Consider how well you get along with your neighbors. If you think your friendship can survive the canine serenade that will come from your house every time the mailman comes, the fire whistle blows, someone walks down the street or another dog barks within a five-mile radius, you might be ready to get a puppy.

10) Dig holes in your lawn directly in the paths where you normally walk. If you can maneuver through your yard in the dark without spraining your ankle, you might be ready to get a puppy.

11) Shred the upholstery on your couch, chairs and recliners. If you think your living room furniture looks better this way, you might be ready to get a puppy.

12) Sprinkle dog hair on all of the food you eat and in every beverage you drink. If you find that your meals taste better with fur as a condiment, you might be ready to get a puppy.

I told my friend that in exchange for the trouble a new puppy brings, she'll get love, companionship, security and more joy than she can imagine. But a dog is not for everyone.

Of course, I'm a pet lover, so I'm biased. As I sit here writing, Scout is asleep at my feet and our cat Murphy is curled up on my lap. Our new puppy, Bandit, is...wait, where is Bandit? And how did the laundry end up in my office?

2
Going For Gold In My Sleep

I've never been known for my athletic abilities, but after watching the last Winter Olympic Games, I've decided to begin training in the hope that my favorite sport will be added in time for the next Winter Games.

Known as Extreme Napping, this highly technical event mixes skill, determination and the benefits of training to honor the competitor with the ability to sleep the longest and most soundly amidst the greatest number of distractions.

Here are some of the things that an extreme napper needs in order to be successful:

The right environment

Skiers can't ski when the snow is slushy and ice dancers can't dance when the ice is bumpy. Likewise, extreme nappers can't nap when the couch is lumpy.

The best napping condition should include a dark, quiet room and a comfortable sofa or bed. But as we all know, during competition the fans are yelling, the sportscasters are commentating and the weather is providing unfavorable conditions, so it's important for an extreme napper to train in a variety of environments. That way, when the chips are down, she can keep her eyes closed, her breathing in check and hopefully take home the Gold for her local Mommy and Me group.

To prepare, try napping during business meetings, in line at the grocery store and while your seven-year-old is poking you in the head to tell you the cat has finished his spin cycle in the washing machine.

The right equipment

In order to block out the maximum amount of distraction, an extreme napper should always have at her disposal a pair of earplugs and an eye mask. Practice using your earplugs in a variety of situations, like when your husband is trying to explain why *People Magazine* isn't a legitimate grocery expense in the family budget.

An extreme napper also needs a warm blankie and a fluffy pillow. If possible, carry your blankie and pillow everywhere you go; that way you can be ready to nap at a moment's notice, like when you're waiting in line at the bank or at the DMV.

The right outfit

Olympic athletes have outfits designed not just for function but for fashion, reflecting both the spirit of the sport and the personality of the competitor.

Consider the outfits of the 2010 Winter Olympics. Whether you're a fan of faux fur, like figure skater Johnny Weir, you prefer the sagging pants and hoodies of the women's snowboarding team, or your tastes run to the extreme, like the aboriginal ice dancing costumes of Russian skaters Shabalin and Domnina, it's important to outfit yourself with a uniform that meets your needs.

Ideally, your outfit should be designed for comfort first, and include a t-shirt, pants with an elastic waistband and a pair of warm slippers. But if you need sequins to get into the napping mood, by all means, glitter away.

The right story

During Olympic coverage, commentators love to share heart-wrenching profiles of athletes who have overcome seemingly insurmountable obstacles on their way to the podium, so it's never too early to start building your backstory.

Keep a journal chronicling the ups and downs of your extreme napping career. Include entries like, "Fell asleep while driving; ended up in Canada," and "Fell asleep in church; husband said snoring drowned out choir." Be sure to include earlier competition failures like, "Originally tried out for women's curling team, but didn't know how to use a broom." If you can connect with viewers on an emotional level and even get them to squeeze out a few tears, your face may end up on a cereal box - even if you don't take home a gold medal.

And remember, if you can also manage to get your spouse and kids dressed in clean clothes and waving flags that aren't made from items in your lingerie drawer, the network will be more likely to broadcast your story, and their smiling faces, around the globe.

The right training schedule

An extreme napper needs practice, so make sure to take advantage of prime daily training opportunities, like napping during dinner or in the shower. Remember, the more you practice, the more proficient you'll become.

I know what you're thinking: chances are slim that the event will be added in time for the next Winter Games. But I figure if they can turn a simple household chore like sweeping into the Olympic sport of curling, anything's possible.

3
Paws, Claws and Deep Dog Breaths

I'm lying on my back, eyes closed, arms at my side, as the DVD directs me to relax and breathe deeply.

As a general rule, I don't exercise. I did join a gym, once, taking advantage of a free month-long trial membership at a new facility that opened near my house. I wanted to take a Pilates class, but when I found out the group met at 6:30 a.m. my body went into total revolt.

"We don't need no stinking Pilates class," my thighs growled.

"Hey, I'm off the clock until 8:30 a.m.," my brain shouted.

My hips creaked, my back whined and my knees protested until I had no choice but to nix the pre-dawn workout.

Unfortunately, I've been having some problems with my back, the result of too many hours sitting at the computer and too few hours doing any other physical activity. My doctor warned me that if I don't do something now, I'm in for some really serious problems down the road. So I made a New Year's Resolution to get in shape.

That's why I'm lying on my living room floor in the middle of the afternoon, cursing my aging body and following along with a Pilates DVD.

The virtual instructor is droning softly - "Feel the breath coming into the body, feel the breath exiting the body" - when all of the sudden I feel warm dog breath on my face and open my eyes to find Scout standing over me, his nose just inches from mine. We make eye contact, and before I can react he's slobbering all over my face, sticking his tongue in my eyes, my nose, my mouth.

I pause the DVD so I can catch my breath, and Scout lies down at my feet, licking my toes. I readjust myself around the dog, the dog toys, the piles of books and the laundry basket (someone really needs to clean this house) and hit the remote.

"Take a deep breath in, and raise your arms over your head for a full body stretch," the instructor croons.

I raise my arms over my head and am shocked to feel sandpaper rubbing my armpit. Wait, it's the cat's tongue.

I push him away, but Murphy lunges at my head, digging his claws into my ponytail and entangling himself in my hair. When I yelp, Scout jumps to my rescue, and I am caught in the middle of a cat and dog wrestling match.

By the time I've separated the two warring pets, the DVD has moved on to the next section of exercises. I pick up as the instructor and her students are demonstrating an abdominal crunch with a twist.

I put one hand behind my head, the other arm at my side (Murphy lunges at my fingers; Scout licks my ear) and raise my upper body (Murphy jumps onto my chest; Scout jumps at Murphy). I lower my body back to the floor (Murphy is under my head; Scout is on my head) and exhale slowly (both Murphy and Scout are licking my face; good grief, this cat has bad breath).

I hit "pause" and wait, not moving. The two finish bathing my face and each other in animal spit. Scout stretches out next to me and sighs deeply. Murphy quietly curls up against my neck.

I hit "play" and resume my exercises, trying not to jostle my companions. I skip the crunches, rationalizing that the five minutes I spent battling the animals has to count for something. I complete my workout with the relaxing cool down (you've got to love an exercise routine that involves simply lying on the floor and breathing) and turn off the DVD player.

I close my eyes and lie still. While the exercises leave me feeling surprisingly energized, the warm dog against my side and the cat purring softly in my ear envelope me in peace.

I softly breath in, softly breath out.

You know, this exercise thing isn't such a bad idea after all.

4
Big Lies About Valentine's Day
by Bandit

Maybe you have heard that February is the month of love because Valentine's Day happens in this month. That is the day when people are supposed to go around telling other people how much they love them and maybe they try to get people to fall in love with them.

But it is all a big lie. Really, they are trying to kill you!

First, a naked baby named Cupid flies around with a bow and arrow trying to shoot people in the heart. Where I live, babies are not allowed to fly around without their mommies (or their diapers), and they are definitely not allowed to play with bows and arrows.

Plus, just in case you didn't know, if you shoot someone through the heart with an arrow they will die. And they probably won't love you for it, either.

People also give presents for Valentine's Day, like chocolate and flowers. They may look nice and pretty but if you get chocolates and flowers, watch out! Someone is trying to poison you.

If a dog eats chocolate he will get emergency poop, and if he eats flowers he will also get a really bad belly ache and get sick and barf. And if he eats them both, he will definitely be going to the animal hospital.

I don't know if chocolate gives people emergency poop, but I would not take a chance. And I don't know if people eat flowers, either. But I have met some people who are not very smart, so I would not be surprised if they did.

Some people also give a very special present called "a rock." A rock is a shiny glass stone that girls like to wear on their finger and it costs about eleventy million dollars. I don't think a rock is a very good present. But I heard about a dog this week who ate 100 rocks, so he must have a lot of girlfriends.

There is also a lot of hugging and kissing on Valentine's Day.

Blech!

First of all, most people who hug you are really trying to strangle you. Why else would they wrap their arms around you and keep squeezing while you are gakking with your tongue hanging out of your mouth?

Second, you can get a lot of germs by kissing. Especially if you kiss my stupid dog sister Bailey, because she eats poop. That is some germy love.

I would tell you more about Valentine's Day except I am very sad because I miss my brother, Scout. He just got out of his dog body and got into his angel body and went to live on God's Farm in the Sky.

If you want to know about love, you should learn more about God's Farm. In heaven, all of the dogs and cats and rabbits and birds and every other animal who ever got sick and died go to live there. They are all happy and no one is in pain and they get to romp and run around and have play time all day. And at night, all of the dogs get to climb up on Jesus' bed to snuggle, and He doesn't even care if their muddy paws get the sheets dirty.

That is love!

I am glad that God has a special place for animals and that he made Scout feel better from his cancer. I think Scout probably likes having angel wings. Maybe he can tell Cupid to stop being naughty and to just play bubbles with God's puppies so we can have a safe Valentine's Day.

Love,
BANDIT!

5
Do You Have A Receipt For That?

I know that receipt is around here somewhere.

I remember when we left the furniture store David told me to put it someplace safe. Which I did. Except now I can't remember where that safe place is.

The receipt is for six bookshelves purchased last summer when we cleaned and reorganized my office, "cleaned and reorganized" being a euphemism for "moved everything around so that now I can't find anything."

The IRS says that to write off the shelves as an office expense I need to provide proof of the purchase.

Well, duh. The shelves are right there in the office. I can't find the receipt but I can take a picture and submit it with my tax return, if that would help.

While I can't prove exactly how much I paid for them, I'm pretty sure each shelf was $45, because frankly they're not worth any more than that. Does the IRS really think I'm going to try and take a deduction for something I can't prove I actually bought? I'm not a liar.

And why would I claim to have overpaid for some cheap furniture? I'm an American female with finely honed bargain shopping skills, thank you very much.

While we're at it, why do I need to prove that I purchased shelves that I can see and touch, but I don't have to prove mileage? Sure, I keep a record of where I went and how many miles I drove, but that doesn't actually prove, for example, those six times last year I met my editor for lunch or that we talked about anything work-related.

I mean, I *did* meet my editor for lunch, and we *did* talk about work, but I don't have to provide a note from the barista or a transcript of the conversation, right? I just add up all the miles I drove and give them to Joe the Accountant. He taps his adding machine and comes up with a deduction amount. He doesn't ask me where I went or what I did while I was there or if anyone can prove my whereabouts on the afternoon of October 15, 2012.

And why don't they even allow you to write off important things? If I ran the IRS I'd allow writers to take deductions for any mood enhancing products used to treat writer's block, like coffee, tea, alcohol (whether purchased in a bar or for home consumption), cigarettes (even though I don't smoke I'd at least like the option), chocolate, ice cream, anything with whipped cream, red toenail polish, psychiatric expenses, anxiety medications and sessions in the tanning booth.

Unfortunately I don't run the IRS, so if I want to get my taxes done on time I really need to find that stupid receipt. I wonder if they'd believe me if I said the cat ate it? I can offer a hairball as proof.

6
Beauty Is Soul Deep

If someone had told me in my 20s that I'd be dealing with facial hair in my 40s, I never would have believed them. Not only does female facial hair sound like something from a horror novel, but in my 20s I had already vowed never to become one of "those" women.

You know who I'm talking about. Those women who go to the grocery store in unmatched sweat suits, who look like they haven't seen a tube of mascara in a decade or bothered to brush their hair in a week. Women more concerned with the price of hamburger than the fact that their gray roots are showing; women who, in their heyday, probably cared about their appearance but who, in their middle years, simply gave up.

"Never!" I vowed.

I'm not sure when the transformation happened, but I remember when I noticed it. I was baking cookies and getting ready to watch "American Idol." With just 15 minutes till show time, I mixed together the sugar, butter and eggs and then realized I was out of vanilla. Rats.

I live just minutes from the grocery and I knew I could drive there and be back in time to finish the dough and get a tray of cookies into the oven before the first contestant hit the stage.

I threw on my coat and ran out the door. It took less than two minutes to get to the store and another two minutes to hit the baking aisle. I grabbed what I needed and flew to the checkout only to find one lane open, with several people ahead of me.

I took my place in line and looked down to scan the titles in the magazine rack. That's when I realized I was wearing two different colored socks.

I knew I was wearing two different colored socks because I was also wearing a pair of olive green sweat pants that I'd bought in high school, pants that were now several inches too short and offered a clear view of my ankles.

I breathed a sigh of relief. At least no one could see my sweatshirt, which was stained with butter and covered in flour, because I was wearing my pea green coat.

I looked like an asparagus.

I reached up to touch my face - I was wearing my glasses, which meant that I probably wasn't wearing any make up. Had I even brushed my hair that day?

That's when it hit me: I'd become one of "those" women.

What surprised me most wasn't the fact that I'd actually gone out in public looking like I'd just rolled out from under the couch. It was that I didn't care.

See, in my 20s, when I made my vow, I looked good on the outside, but inside I was a mess. Lonely, confused, feeling unloved and trying desperately to control the slowly unraveling pieces of my life.

Now, in my 40s, I was beginning to realize that I'm beautiful on the inside, even if I was a mess on the outside.

I'd learned an important lesson: My worth and beauty aren't determined by my hair or my clothes. The Creator of the Universe formed me in His own image. When God looks at me, He sees beautiful.

I admit that I was a little embarrassed that I'd run out of the house without looking in the mirror. But I didn't let it get to me. I wasn't worthless. I wasn't ugly. I was just, well, messy.

Sure, I dye my gray roots and pluck those random facial hairs and usually go out in public dressed in clean clothes. But I've learned that nothing I can do on the outside can change how I feel on the inside.

Because beauty isn't skin deep. It's soul deep. And maybe that's a lesson that can only come with age.

7
You've Been Shopped!

My sister has the greatest job in the world: she's a member of the Mystery Shopping Police.

Usually I wouldn't be able to talk about this without having to kill you afterwards for fear of blowing her cover, but since she lives in another state, I think we're safe. But be warned: if you let the cat out of the bag, she's coming after you with a price sticker gun.

Several times a day my sister goes into stores, restaurants, gas stations, banks and other businesses to make a purchase, return an item, have a meal or do some other typical transaction. She looks like a normal customer, with her coupons and shopping list, but she's really on assignment from the Mystery Shopping Police. After she leaves the store, she immediately reports her findings to Headquarters, and within a week you know whether or not you've passed inspection.

It's a power I'd like to have when I'm on the receiving end of particularly poor service, like when I'm standing at the grocery check-out and my cashier is busy talking to the cashier in the next line about her impending date with the captain of the football team. She's discussing lipstick flavors while ignoring the fact that she's putting the gallon of milk on top of the loaf of bread. I'd love to be able to make a citizen's shopping arrest, or at least write a citation for rude and ignorant customer service.

We recently went to a popular chicken place for take-out. We waited in a long line to place our order, and then stood with the other customers in a long line waiting for our food. Order after order came up for people who were ahead of us in line, then for people who had been behind us in line. After what seemed like hours, the cashier noticed us.

"You're waiting for the popcorn shrimp, right?"

"Yes," my husband said. "How much longer is it going to be?"

She tilted her head, arched an eyebrow and, with her hand on her hip, replied, "It takes three minutes to cook."

I pointed to the clock. "It's been *17 minutes* since you took our order."

"Well, there are other customers ahead of you," she snapped, and stomped off to the back room.

Right then, I wished I had a Mystery Shopping Police badge. I would have whipped it out, held it high for all of the other customers to see and shouted, "Hold it right there, missy!"

She would have seen the badge and shaken in her rubber-soled, regulation, fast-food-chain sneakers. Oh, I'll bet then I'd get my popcorn shrimp in three minutes or less.

"It doesn't work that way," my sister explained to me when I recounted the story the next day. "You have to remain anonymous. That way, you get a realistic picture of their service."

But I don't want a realistic picture of their service. I want good service.

In the end, I don't suppose I would make a good Mystery Shopping Police Officer. I'd probably let the power go to my head and go around town demanding that waiters pay attention to me and that cashiers charge me the right amount for my groceries. I'd insist that stock clerks know which aisle the marshmallows are in and that restaurants train their servers not to play with their hair and then touch my silverware.

But I guess I'll have to rely on my sister to keep the stores safe for shoppers like me. Thank goodness she can keep a secret.

8
There Is Life After High School

Each June, thousands of fresh-faced high school seniors walk across the stage to accept their diplomas, then head off to make their mark in the big, big world.

It's been - well, let's just say a very long time since I graduated from high school - and the world was a different place back then. Shoulder pads were in, for example, along with big hair, blue eyeliner and disco music.

I've learned a lot since then and not all of it about fashion. Being older, wiser and more experienced, I thought I'd share some of the tidbits of wisdom I've picked up over the last few decades.

Don't get stuck in high school

High school is just a teeny portion of your life. If the last four years were a nightmare, forget about them, because the best is yet to come.

Well, for most people anyway. Someone once told me that those popular, hot-shot classmates who made the rest of us feel so insignificant actually peaked in high school, and that the geeks would get their revenge at the first class reunion. I didn't believe it then, but trust me, they were right.

Even if you felt dorky or invisible in high school, or if those four years were marked with insecurity and pain, as the years roll on you'll see yourself and those classmates through new eyes. Someday your grown up self will face your high school self with clarity and grace and confidence.

And don't forget that time is the great equalizer. Everyone gets older, everyone gets fatter, everyone gets grayer or balder or richer or poorer or happier or more miserable.

College is an option, not an obligation or a right

Society has put a lot of pressure on students to go straight to college right after high school and a lot of additional emphasis on pursuing white collar, professional careers. But while Americans revere lawyers and doctors and corporate CEOs, never forget that it's the garbage men and sewer workers and auto mechanics who keep the country functioning. No one on Wall Street would be working if the streets were knee-deep in garbage and, well, you know what.

In fact, college is sometimes overrated. Learning a trade, if that's where your interests lie, may actually offer a more stable career than say, obtaining a Bachelor's or Master's Degree. In times of economic crisis, auto mechanics and hair stylists and roofers and plumbers are always in demand. Not necessarily so for stockbrokers - or Art History majors.

College may be overrated, but education is not
Whether or not you go on to college, learn a trade, or just head into the work force, never stop learning. Read the books you were supposed to read in high school. Watch documentaries. Learn more about topics that interest you. Take a class. Try something new.

Education is a lifestyle. You don't need to pursue a degree to learn. Learn for the sake of expanding your mind and understanding your world. The quest for knowledge is a journey that should never end.

Things can always be worse
No matter how terrible your life may seem, don't forget there is always someone in more dire straits than you are - physically, emotionally, spiritually and financially.

There may come a day when you feel like you've hit rock bottom. When that happens, think of a few things in life that would be worse than your current situation. And when you've thought of those things, remember that there is someone suffering right now.

Then reach out to those people in need. Lend a hand. Buy some groceries. Give a hug. Offer a few dollars. Share a kind word. You're never so low that you can't reach out to help someone else who's struggling.

Knowledge is never wasted

Surprise! You actually will use those math skills in real life! Finding the area of a rectangle may have seemed like a waste of time, but when you buy your first home and need to figure out how many 1 ft. square tiles you need to cover a kitchen floor shaped like an octagon, you'll wish you'd pay more attention in Geometry class.

Every day is a do-over

And lastly, let me share a piece of advice from that sage philosopher, Scarlett O'Hara: "Tomorrow is another day."

Don't dwell on the past. Move forward with the joy and expectation that you were created for a purpose and that God is going to do something grand with your life. His mercies really are new every morning.

9
Being Successful At Being 40-Something

If one more person uses the phrase "women your age," especially in relation to my hair, my weight or my eyesight, someone is going to get hurt.

Seriously.

I've been told that my hair is difficult to control lately because "women my age" have fluctuating hormones that affect our hair. Well, hormones and coarse, wiry gray hair.

I can't lose weight because, apparently, "women my age" just naturally tend to carry more body fat around our middles and in our behinds.

Those sagging upper arms? They're just something most "women my age" have difficulty getting rid of.

The reason I need bifocals is because, when you're "my age," the muscles in your eyes don't respond as quickly to changes in distance as they used to.

And if you believe the TV commercials, it doesn't seem like things are going to get any better: Bladder leakage, hair loss, dentures. Surely women over 40 do more than just fall apart piece by piece?

I did a Google search for "successful women over 40" and came up mainly with sites explaining how to get pregnant and how to get a date. With the bad eyesight, extra pounds and gray hair that comes with being 40-something, it's no wonder women my age aren't getting much action. And the ones that get the attention do so because they look great "for their age."

In other words, it seems like the only thing notable a woman over 40 can hope to achieve is a youthful complexion or a pregnancy, and neither one without cosmetic or medical intervention. I'm starting to think that the best years of my life are behind me.

Then my writing friend Steve told me about Eudora Welty. Her first short story was published when she was in her late 20s and her first book at 32, but she was 64 when she won the Pulitzer Prize for her novel, *The Optimist's Daughter*. Her career was just taking off when she was my age and her greatest success was decades away.

Then there's Mother Teresa. While she took her vows at age 20, she was 40 when she founded the Missionaries of Charity, caring for the sick and dying in India as well as becoming a voice for peace around the world. In 1982, for example, during the Siege of Beirut, Mother Teresa brokered a temporary cease-fire between the Israeli army and the Palestinian guerrillas in order to rescue 37 children trapped in a hospital on the front lines. She was 72 at the time.

New York Times best-selling author Lillian Jackson Braun wrote the first book in her famous "The Cat Who" series in 1966 - when she was in her 50s. She followed it with two more novels, in 1967 and 1968, and didn't publish another book for 18 years. Then, in 1986, she resumed the series, going on to publish dozens more best-sellers that sold millions of copies and were translated into 16 languages. She died in 2011 at the age of 97; her final book had been published just four years earlier.

Look at Grandma Moses. Her painting career didn't even *begin* until she was in her 70s. I guess some women over 40 are just beginning to tap into their creative and intellectual abilities.

And not just famous women, either. My mom (who by the way went totally gray decades ago and has refused to color her hair because she likes it that way) could never be accused of being old. Now in her 70s, she's got the mindset of a 20-year-old. She works full time, has an active social life (including online) and is full of spunk.

As for me, I may not go on to win a Pulitzer Prize, make a significant contribution to the art world, land on the New York Times best-seller list or broker world peace. But that doesn't mean I'm useless. Maybe my best years are still ahead of me.

As my other writing friend Phil said after reading the draft for this column, "See, women your age do have a lot to offer the world."

Of course, I had to punch him.

10
But I Can Explain

It's the first day of first grade and the bright classroom is filled with eager students. I sit at my desk as the teacher, barely out college, calls the roll, gently sounding out names which are answered with a "here" by the sweet faces around me.

She finishes with the Zs and asks, "Is there anyone whose name I didn't call?"

I raise my hand.

"What's your last name, dear?"

"Keltz," I answer, embarrassed as all eyes are on me, because we're all sure I'm in the wrong room, and even first graders know when to savor someone else's pain.

"Oh! I did call your name sweetheart." She smiles and puts a checkmark on her list. "Elizabeth J. Keltz."

"No, my name isn't Elizabeth," I reply, frightened, because I'm the center of attention, and pleased, because

I am the center of attention, and curious, because someone else in the room has the same last name as me. "I'm Joanne."

"I see," she says with a puzzled look on her face, and calls the office secretary, who calls my mother, only to find out that in fact, I am Elizabeth J. Keltz - the "J" being Joanne.

Now I'm puzzled, because I'm pretty sure no one ever told me that.

I've redeemed myself as the kid who couldn't find the right classroom, but am now forever pegged as the first grader who doesn't know her own name. What a stupid head.

"So, Elizabeth, what should we call you?" the gentle teacher asks. "Beth, maybe?"

"No, my name is Joanne," I insist.

All eyes are on me again. Her name is Elizabeth but we call her Joanne? Why not Beth? Why not Liz? Why not Betsy or Liza, or Sam or Bob for that matter?

It is a scene I am doomed to repeat over and over throughout my life, every first day of the new school year, every job interview, every time I need to make a legal transaction. It keeps me on my toes, because I have to constantly remember who I am in every situation.

The teller at the bank calls me "Beth," for example, because all of my banking is done in my legal first name; I need to remember to respond or I'll stand there holding up the line. My doctor calls me "Elizabeth" (ok, let's keep that professional).

Almost everyone else calls me "Joanne," except for a few select family members who insist on calling me "Jo" (and whom I have decided not to kill until they're millionaires and I'm sure I'm included in their wills).

I have a hard time keeping it straight myself. I had to call our mortgage company the other day. After I gave the customer service representative the account number, she said, "I just need to verify some information. What's your name?"

"Joanne Brokaw. I mean, the account is under Elizabeth Brokaw."

Silence.

"See, I go by my middle name but the account is under my real name."

Silence.

"I mean, Joanne *is* my real name, too, but my first name..."

Sigh.

"Can I just verify my social security number?"

I'm obviously suffering from some weird split personality disorder. It might explain why I can perform tasks for which I seem clearly not qualified while at the same time fail at tasks that I should be able to handle in my sleep.

It explains why, for example, I can handle all of our household finances even though I can never add 2 and 2 and get less than 5 (Elizabeth is good at math), and why I am always down to the wire on deadline despite the fact that I've written 99% of the piece weeks before (Joanne is a creative procrastinator).

It probably explains why, when I'm at a screening or media event (Elizabeth gets invited to all the good parties), I prefer to talk to the waiters and waitresses rather than the celebrities (Joanne likes to socialize in her own income bracket).

It's why I can get up in front of an audience and speak coherently on almost any topic without hesitation (Elizabeth can work a crowd), but can't call customer service to discuss my cell phone bill without breaking down in tears (Joanne has some emotional issues).

And it is the reason why, after more than 40 years, I find myself continually having to explain almost everything I do and say. I'm confused; why shouldn't you be, too?

"Yes, I know it sounds like I called you a jackass based on what Bob told you I said, but if you were there you would understand that I really meant was..."

"I know I said I'd be there on Monday, but I meant next Monday, because I couldn't possibly have been there this Monday, since I don't think I called until Tuesday..."

"Oh, when you said I could completely take over the task, I thought that meant I could print out the budget projections on purple paper..."

"No, officer, I know that it looks like we're all drunk because the passengers are hanging out the windows and I crossed the center line, but honest, I'm really sober..."

It would be simple to blame my parents. They gave me this confusing identity, after all. But even after all these years I can't get a straight answer out of either of them on whose bright idea it was to give me one name and then call me something else.

"Your mother wanted all of our names to start with Js," my father, Jim, says about my mother, Judy, referring also to my sister, Jackie. (My father, by the way, is now remarried to a woman whose name does not start with J.)

"Your father wanted to name you after his mother," my mother counters, "but I didn't like the name Josephine. So we compromised. Your first name, Elizabeth, is my mother's middle name, and your middle name, Joanne, is for your other grandmother's first name."

"Besides," she adds, "I wanted to call you Beth, but your father wouldn't let me."

Well, now. That explains a lot, doesn't it?

11
Confessions of an Office Supply Addict

I have a confession to make: I'm an addict - an office supply addict.

I have an abnormal addiction to pens, paper, mechanical pencils, notepads, journals - you name it. I rarely walk out of a store without having purchased some sort of stationary item - paper clips, file folders or a snazzy new pen.

I have a notebook in every room in my house, one in my car and one in my purse, just in case I have a story idea and can't make it to my desk before I forget it. I usually have a pen tucked behind my ear or stuck in my ponytail, even if I'm going out in public. When I see a blank journal that I find attractive I buy it, even though I couldn't fill the ones I already have if I wrote for two hours, every day for the next ten years. I keep a supply of pocket folders in a range of colors to suit my every mood. I have a panic attack if I can't find my stapler.

I think it has something to do with the back-to-school sales. I remember as a kid getting ready for the new school year, the smell of autumn and new possibilities in the air, my book bag filled with folders, freshly sharpened pencils and clean, college-ruled notebook paper just begging to be filled with stories, notes and essays.

Every September, I would vow that this would be the year I would stay organized. This year, I would put the science notes in the science folder and the English notes in the English folder. This year, I would save all of the quizzes so I could study for the cumulative final. This year, I would record every homework assignment in my pocket calendar and never again be scrambling at the last minute to complete a project.

But it always ended the same. In less than a month, I had geometry theorems mixed in with grammar notes. I would show up to science class without my textbook ("Wait," I'd ask, "isn't this supposed to be health class?") and had taken to writing homework assignments on my hands (I had the first Palm Pilot). My locker always looked like a tornado had blown through a paper factory.

It's more than twenty years later and I'm still not organized. I have trays on my desk for current files, yet I'm continually digging through the towering pile of folders under my chair to find what I need for the day.

I have a three-tiered bin on wheels to hold the projects waiting to be reviewed, yet the press kits overflow onto the floor and under the desk. (I think they breed when I turn out the lights.)

I have plastic bins, desktop organizers, filing cabinets and shelves, and I still have to hunt for paper clips, Scotch tape, computer paper and rubber bands. I have three calendars within arm's reach, but I never know what day it is.

I try. I really do.

A few months ago, I designated a spiral notebook for each publication I write for, a place where I could record notes, ideas and assignments for each magazine and not get everything mixed up. When I sat down to write this column, I opened the corresponding magazine's notebook and found a recipe for candied pecans (I don't even like pecans), a phone number with the notation "Do not lose!" and pages of paw prints that appear to be some sort of coded message from the cat. But no notes or column ideas.

But that's OK. In September, when school and office supplies are on sale, I'm really going to get organized. All I need first is a new box of fine point pens and a fresh legal pad. Oh, and some paper clips...and another box of manila folders...

12
Treat Your Spouse Like A Dog

I read an article recently in which a psychologist suggested that if we treated our spouses like we treat our pets, we'd have better relationships with the people we love. In the piece, the good doctor explains that in her counseling sessions with couples she says she often hears that partners "wish to receive the kind of love and attention the pet is getting."

Well, if she's sure that's what we're supposed to do.

From now on I'll make my husband sit quietly and then shake my hand before I give him dinner. When he does something I want him to do, I'll give him a cookie. And when he starts to get on my last nerve, I'll lock him in a crate for a time out.

I'm kidding. Sort of. I mean, the doctor does have a point. Sometimes the people closest to us get the short end of the stick when it comes to our time and affection. Every day we'll tell our dogs how much we love them, how great we think they are and how happy they make us, while we wait for a Hallmark holiday to tell our spouse the same thing.

When the dog refuses to come when called we get mad but get over it quickly, because really, who can resist those cute puppy eyes? But when your spouse is late for dinner (again) and forgets to call (again), he gets the cold shoulder for the rest of the night. When you come home from work and are greeted at the door by your cat, who wraps himself around your legs because he missed you while you were gone, you get all mushy inside and cuddle the fluffy feline, no matter how tired you are. When you greet your wife after a long day at the office, you barely say hello.

We've convinced ourselves that our pets shower us with love and expect nothing in return, while the humans in our life always seem to need something from us. So we think that it's easier to love a dog or a cat and much more difficult to maintain healthy relationships with people. But think about it. When was the last time your spouse barfed in your purse? Ate your socks? Peed on the living room rug? Bit the mailman? Rolled around in mud and then jumped on the bed?

The truth is that our pets demand much of our time and energy, but we forgive them their faults because we're focused on the positive things they bring to our lives. Which I guess is the point of the article.

The cat will turn his nose up today at the food he loved yesterday, and we'll spend whatever it costs to find something he'll eat. So when your husband turns his nose up at the casserole he loved so much last week, maybe we should write it off as a fussy moment and happily make him a sandwich. When the dog is nudging our arm for the umpteenth time in an hour, begging for us to get up and play catch, we'll gladly oblige. So when your wife needs a few minutes of your undivided attention, even if it's to discuss something that doesn't interest you in the least, maybe it's time to turn off the TV or put down the cell phone and listen to what she has to say.

But if things get really bad, there's always the dog crate.

13

Insomnia

It's after midnight and I can't sleep.

I have a column due in the morning and I have no idea what I'm going to write about, so I keep turning over thoughts in my head. The problem is that the column ideas are being pushed aside by weightier items demanding my attention.

Take the fortune cookie I ate today.

When I cracked it open, I was stunned to see that my fortune said, "Ganaras mucho dinero." The translation on the other side: "You will earn a lot of money."

Earn a lot of money? Do you know what humor columnists are paid? And why was my Chinese fortune in Spanish? (And where were my lucky numbers?)

Were these cookies destined for a Chinese restaurant in Mexico and intercepted on the black market before they landed on my grocery store shelf? Are they irregular cookies (which would explain why they were on sale)? And if so, I hope they were safe to eat, since I ate the whole box. (And yes, all of the fortunes were in Spanish.)

These are the things that keep me up at night.

Here's another one: Before I go to bed, I jot down in my journal some notes about the day - what I did, where I went, who irritated me, what Bandit ate and then barfed up. I noticed tonight that my handwriting today looks nothing like my handwriting in yesterday's entry or the day's before, which got me thinking.

What if my Spanish fortune cookie comes true and I make a lot of money as a famous writer and a hundred years from now my great-great-grandchildren take my journals to the "Antiques Roadshow" and the experts deem them fake because they think the entries were written by more than one person?

Even I can't read my own writing sometimes, so how can I expect a complete stranger to decipher my chicken scratch? My poor great-great-grandchildren. Robbed of their inheritance, all because I have bad handwriting.

Does anyone use a key to open their car door anymore? Don't we all have those little beepy things? So why do they still make lock de-icer?

And while I'm on the subject, what happens if Bandit manages to eat my car keys, something he attempts several times a day? When I want to unlock my car, will I have to squeeze the dog until he beeps?

Who determines the sizes on women's clothing? How come I can fit into a size 8 from one store but have to wear a size 12 from another store? Making the clothing bigger and labeling it with a smaller size does not satisfy my ego; it just means that when I try on clothes I have to try on three sizes of the same item, which takes three times as long and leaves me three times as frustrated.

How does the mailman get his own mail? Is it delivered to "Jimmy at the Post Office" or does it get delivered to his house? Does he deliver his own mail, and if not, does he know his mailman's name? Does his mail ever get delivered to the wrong house or get rolled into a ball and shoved into the mail slot, the way it gets delivered to my house whenever Jimmy the Mailman is on vacation?

If I have to get a real job, I wonder if they'd let me train sea lions. I think I would like that job. I'd teach them to clap their flippers every time I walked into the room. I bet that would do a lot for my self-esteem, even if deep down I knew they were only doing it for the fish.

Why does Facebook think it knows so much about me? I took a personality quiz the other day called "Which character on Gilligan's Island are you?" Turns out I am not sultry Ginger or the brilliant Professor, like I had hoped. I'm Gilligan.

And when Facebook posted the results - that I'm a loveable, adorable goofball - everyone agreed that pretty much described me.

Adorable goofball? Is that how I'll be remembered when I die?

Maybe I need to go find someone to yawn in front of me so I can go to sleep. It worked in "Dr. Seuss's Sleep Book." Maybe it will work for me.

After all, I have a column due in the morning and I really need to come up with something to write about.

14

Fit, Green and Squashed

I confess right up front: I wrote this column while I was in the doctor's office waiting for my annual breast squash.

For those of you who aren't familiar with a breast squash, it's a procedure during which a woman's breast is squashed like a pressed flower between a small X-ray table and a glass pane, the two of which are then tightly screwed together like a vise in order to keep the woman from leaving the room should she develop a sudden desire to parade around the doctor's office half-naked.

Once appropriately anchored, the technician takes several X-rays to check for breast cancer. Technically, it's called a mammogram, but we all know it for what it really is: Pain with a co-pay.

This particular doctor recommends women wait for their test results, lest they have to return in a week for another X-ray if it is determined that there is something unusual with the first mammogram, like a lesion is evident or the technician had her finger over the camera lens.

It makes things more convenient for the doctor and reduces the anxiety if you get a call to return for another round of X-rays, but it turns a five-minute procedure into a two-hour appointment.

That's how I ended sitting in a waiting room pretending like it's an everyday event to lounge around with 50 women in bathrobes, drinking (decaffeinated) coffee and watching tropical fish swim around in a 100-gallon tank.

On the bright side, I got to read magazines I can't afford to buy, glossy tomes filled with the latest fashion and health information for trendy, hip women on the go. Being neither hip nor trendy, I enjoy the opportunity to brush up on style and pop culture news.

According to one article on fitness and the environment, for example, I learned that if, instead of driving, I were to walk one mile, three times a week, I could burn 200 extra calories and lose three pounds in one year. Not only that, I'd save eight gallons of gas.

The point of the article was that by burning body fat rather than gasoline a woman could be getting into shape and saving the environment at the same time.

I'm not buying it. If I walk 156 miles a year just so I can lose three pounds and save $33.40 in gas, there had better be lunch with George Clooney waiting at the end of the journey.

As I was working out these numbers in the waiting room the technician called my name and ushered me into a private conference closet to give me the mammogram results.

I felt faint. I was certain she was about to tell me that I was dying from breast cancer, one of my biggest fears (along with brain tumors, heart attack, skin cancer, cavities and dye-resistant gray hair).

"Your mammogram looks fine," she said instead, adding that I could schedule another routine appointment in a year.

Hopefully doctors are working on a way to lose weight that will allow me to save the planet without walking half way around it, and I'll be able to read about it in twelve months when I return for my annual breast squash.

If I start walking now, I could be three whole pounds lighter by then.

15

Happy Halloween!
by Bandit

Today I am going to tell you about a holiday called Halloween. Just in case you didn't know, Halloween is when you dress up in a scary costume and go visit your friends and force them to give you treats. And if they don't give you a treat, you get to play a trick on them! Doesn't that sound like fun?

First, you have to pick out a costume. You should dress up so that no one will know who you are. That way, if you have to play a trick no one will know who did it. Pretty tricky, huh?

It is important to pick a costume that is good for a dog. Some mommies and daddies don't know that dogs talk to each other using our tails and our ears, and if we can't see each other we can't tell if another dog is a friend or a meanie. We can get into fights that way. It is called a mixed up communication.

If you get into a fight with another dog you will have to get a visit from the dog police and get jailed at your house for eleventeen days. You will not get to play in the park and everyone will call you a Bad Dog. So pick a costume that lets your tail and your ears show or you might end up in dog jail and be called a Bad Dog forever.

After you get dressed up in your costume, go to the neighbor's house and ring the doorbell. When they open the door, bark "Trick or treat!!" as loud as you can. Then put on your sad puppy face and say, "Don't you think I'm the cutest thing you ever saw? Don't you want to give me some treats? I'll take some hot dogs and cheese and dog biscuits and two Snickers for Mommy, please."

If they do not give you a treat, you get to play a trick on them! You can pee on their leg or chew up their slippers or chase their cat or sit outside their bedroom window at two o'clock in the morning and bark for a while. I bet that next time they will have some good dog treats when you come to visit.

After you go trick or treating, you should go home and make some popcorn and watch a scary movie with your mommy while you go through your Halloween loot. Hopefully you got lots of good things to eat.

Here is something else you might not know: Dogs should not eat candy, like chocolate or fake sugar or gum or lollypops. So stick to hot dogs and cheese and dog biscuits and give all of the candy to your mommy. Otherwise you might end up with a big tummy ache and have to visit the hospital, which is not fun, because at the hospital they lock you in a cage and stick needles in your legs and suck out all of your blood and do experiments on it and make you wear a lampshade on your head.

I know because it happened to me and I would not lie about it.

While you are at home watching your movie and eating popcorn, you will probably get a lot of visitors at your house. Those are other trick-or-treaters, and you better give them something yummy or they will play a trick back on you!

Sometimes people play very naughty tricks on Halloween and then run away really fast. Here is a secret: if you wear a good costume *people* won't know who you are, but *dogs* have super duper noses. If you play a big trick at a dog's house, even if you are wearing a good costume the dog can still smell who you really are and tell the police!

Ha ha ha ha! Who's the trickster now?

Just so you know, you do not have to bark every time the doorbell rings, but it helps makes the night more exciting.

I hope you have a Happy Halloween!

Your pal,
BANDIT!

16
Mind Reading Mommy

Parenting is a tough job. Not only are you expected to birth another human being, you have to feed, clothe, teach, bathe, chauffeur, discipline and otherwise raise the child so that they become a productive member of society.

Oh, and let's not forget the mind reading.

When my daughter was three years old, we were driving on the expressway, wrapped in our automotive cocoon, when from the back seat I heard her sweet little voice ask, "Mommy, what's that?"

"What's what?" I asked.

"That."

I looked in the rearview mirror to see her sitting in her car seat. She was hugging her teddy bear and pointing out the front windshield.

"Is it inside or outside the car?"

"It's that thing, right there."

I looked ahead as I drove and ventured a guess. "The windshield? This glass that we're looking through?" I reached forward to tap the window.

"No, what's that?"

"The rearview mirror?"

"What's that?"

I pointed to the mirror. "It lets me see what's going on behind me so I don't have to turn around." I peeked back at her.

"No! What's THAT?" She kicked her feet on the back of my seat. Oops, my mistake. Try again.

"Do you mean the trees that we're passing?"

"No, THAT."

"What? What?" I asked, my eyes furtively darting back and forth to scan the sides of the road as I drove.

"What is that thing RIGHT THERE?"

She stabbed the air with her little finger to emphasize the direction she wanted me to look. She was pointing at, well, everything out the front windshield.

"What color is it?" I asked.

"I don't know. What is it?"

"Is it in the car?"

"No. What is it?"

I peeked back to see her still pointing straight ahead. I looked for something unusual that might be prompting this interrogation, my knuckles turning white as I gripped the steering wheel just a little tighter.

"Are you pointing at another car? The building coming up? The bridge? The sign?"

"No. What is THAT thing, right THERE?"

"What, the birds? The clouds? The barn? The lamp post? The guardrail?"

"Mommy. What is THAT?"

I took a breath and ventured one last guess.

"Are you pointing at the air?"

She sighed very loudly.

"Never mind. We passed it."

I thought that once my daughter grew up I could put my mind reading skills to rest. Silly me.

When Cassie was 20, she was living in Florida and flew home one weekend to surprise me. At the end of her visit, I took her to the airport for her flight back to the sunny shores. We said our teary goodbyes at 5:50 a.m. and then I went home to crawl back in bed.

At 7:50 a.m. the phone rang.

"Mom. I'm in Washington and I don't know where to go."

I rubbed my eyes. "Well, I don't know where you need to go. Ask someone who works at the airport."

"There's no one here. I'm going to miss my flight."

I pictured my daughter standing completely alone in one of the nation's busiest airports.

"Look for someone wearing a uniform," I suggested.

"I don't know if the people in uniforms work here or are just pilots going to their flights."

"No, I mean go to the ticket counter and ask for help." Problem solved. I snuggled back under the covers.

"There's no one at the ticket counter. We landed at a Delta gate but I'm flying US Air."

I wasn't sure if that mattered. "Well, any of the ticket agents can tell you how to get to your next gate."

"I don't know what my next gate is. They changed it."

Problem not solved. I sat up in bed. "You need to look for that big bank of television screens and find your flight number on the monitor. That'll tell you what gate to go to."

"MOM. I don't know where to go."

I closed my eyes. Breathe in, breathe out. "When does your flight board?"

"Right now."

"Well, I can't help you from Rochester. You need to find someone who works at the..."

She hung up on me. I sat on the edge of the bed and waited. A few minutes later the phone rang again.

"Mom, so I asked some guy and he looked at my ticket and told me to go to Gate 25."

I sighed with relief. "OK, so your flight's leaving from Gate 25."

"No, the guy at Gate 25 told me to wait here for the shuttle. Am I supposed to get on the shuttle?"

I gripped the phone and tried to stay calm. "I don't know! Ask someone who actually works at the airport!"

"I'm going to miss my flight. What should I do?"

"I DON'T KNOW!"

"Nice, Mom. You don't need to yell."

"Well I can't help you from..."

She hung up on me again.

By now I was in panic mode. If she couldn't manage to get from one gate to another, how was she going to manage if she actually missed her flight? And what could I do from New York?

I dialed her number. Busy.

I tried again and she answered.

"Cassie, when we flew through Reagan last time, I think we had to take the shuttle..."

"Mom, I figured it out."

I sighed and unclenched my grip on the phone. "Good, who was finally able to help?"

"I just called Sarah."

She's stuck in Washington so she calls her friend in Florida? "OK, so do you know what gate you're supposed to be at?"

"No, I haven't figured that out yet."

The more panicked I got, the calmer she sounded.

"When does your plane leave? What are you going to do?"

"I don't know, it leaves pretty soon. I'm fine."

"Do you need to get on the shuttle? Do you know what to do when you get off the shuttle? Do you know where your gate is?"

"Mom! Don't worry about it, OK? Geez."

"Well, are you going to make your plane?"

"I DON'T KNOW!"

She hung up on me. I waited, but she didn't call back. I called her cell phone but it went to voice mail.

Did she make the flight? Was she stranded in Washington? Did she have enough money? What if she got on the wrong flight? Who was picking her up at the airport? Was no news good news?

The next time I heard from her was at noon, when she called to tell me that she was home in Tampa and having lunch with her friends.

Of course, considering my mind reading skills I should have known that already.

17

Puppy Love Is Messy Business

I'm always fascinated by the attempts by toy manufacturers to create playthings that offer a semi-authentic version of reality, an alternate world where plastic food doesn't need refrigeration and babies that cry can be stuffed in the toy box until tomorrow. All the fun of real life without the mess!

One toy that's caught my attention is a plush dog named Biscuit who, according to the ads, "Reacts to humans much like a real golden retriever."

Biscuit follows voice commands like "sit," "beg" and "lie down," just like a real dog. And, the makers tout, "The best part is there's never a mess to clean up!"

Where's the fun in that?

Biscuit can't offer a child the best parts of dog ownership, like a total face-licking after he's had a good, long drink from the toilet. He can't romp across the bedspread with muddy paws or shed all over every piece of clothing the child owns. He can't chew new school shoes or $40 math textbooks, and he certainly can't run up enormous vet bills.

So sad.

See, I'm one of those nutty parents who thinks every kid needs a dog. A real dog, not a bionic one.

Fortunately I married a man who felt the same way, so when our daughter was young we got a puppy, a little ball of Border Collie fur that, when we went to pick out our furry new family member, followed our daughter Cassie around the entire time, tripping on her tiny puppy legs and scrambling to keep up with the girl who would bring her home.

It's debatable whether Cassie picked Natasha or vice versa, but there is no question that the two bonded instantly, like Lassie and Timmy. It was the kind of child/dog relationship dreams are made of.

But did you ever see Timmy scoop up Lassie's poop? Of course not. Timmy romped around the countryside with the brilliant canine while his parents financed the Dog Chow and took care of the dirty work.

I'm actually not opposed to that balance of responsibility. Sure, Cassie fed Natasha every day and brushed her once in a while, but David and I willingly shielded her from the bulk of dirty work (including pooper scooper duty).

Cassie's primary job was to love her dog. In return, Natasha's job was to protect Cassie from all threats real and imagined, including bullies at school and the rogue neighborhood Pomeranian.

Can Biscuit offer that kind of protection? I think not.

That's not to say that Cassie didn't experience the dark side of dog ownership. Natasha had a taste for ballet shoes, particularly the left ones, often leaving our little ballerina barefoot minutes before we had to leave for class. Natasha did the bulk of her shedding in Cassie's room and, when she was sick, she usually threw up all over Cassie's bed.

Biscuit can't teach kids that when you love someone you have to take the good with the bad or that it really is important to put your shoes in the closet.

When Cassie left for college, Natasha and I comforted each other on those long days when we missed our girl. When I started working from home, she kept my feet warm while I was at the computer and nudged me with her cold nose to remind me when it was time to take a break.

I don't think Biscuit can give that kind of comfort, even if he is soft and plush.

Biscuit would be a better toy if, when you told him to sit, he barked, or if, when you told him to lie down, he chased the cat. He'd be more lovable if, after you hugged him, you were covered from head to toe in dog fur or if he peed on the living room carpet once in a while, just to keep things interesting.

The description of Biscuit says, "This sweet sidekick is sure to become your new best friend."

I have to disagree.

Dog is not man's best friend because he responds to every command like a robot. Dog is man's best friend because he protects and loves us, even when we're not very loveable.

Besides, the price tag for Biscuit is $179. For that, you could go to the animal shelter and rescue a real live dog that would happily shed on your furniture and chew your shoes and truly love you for the rest of his life.

18

Flying the Friendly (and Expensive) Skies

Let's be clear about one thing: I'm not an aeronautical expert. I can't figure out how a plane flies without flapping its wings like a bird, so it should come as no surprise that I don't understand the airline policies about luggage.

If you've traveled by plane you know that most airlines, in an effort to offset rising fuel costs, are now charging passengers anywhere from $25 to $100 to check a second suitcase.

I'm notorious for over packing.

If I'm going to be away for two days at a writing conference, I need to bring at least four pair of shoes, three pair of pajamas, and at least six pair of underwear. I need to be prepared for every possible social gathering (formal, semi-formal, business casual) and every possible emergency (stranded in a storm, flight diverted to Tibet). I need my hair dryer, curling iron, flat iron; I bring my own toiletries. I carry a change of clothing in my carry on, in case my luggage gets lost, along with snacks, in case I get hungry on the way. I bring at least two books, because I never know what I'll be in the mood to read. And, if I still have room, I bring my own pillow.

Needless to say, the change in airline luggage policies put a serious cramp in my ability to travel comfortably.

Even if I manage to stuff everything into one suitcase, I still need to meet the baggage weight requirements. Coming home from a writing conference, I had to leave behind ten pounds of sample magazines or else incur a $25 charge because my bag was overweight.

I thought maybe the airlines were encouraging passengers to pack lightly so the planes would weigh less and therefore use less gas. But on a recent flight, our take-off was delayed so the crew could add ballast to the plane, because, as the pilot happily informed us, the passengers "didn't check enough luggage."

Excuse me?

Did you want me to check a second suitcase or not? Because I had a lot of stuff I could have packed if I knew you needed more weight. I just didn't want to pay $25 to haul three pair of black boots (high heel, low heel, flat heel), two sweaters (white, off-white) and three pair of jeans (skinny, boot cut, relaxed fit) through the friendly skies, just in case I changed my mind about what I wanted to wear while I was in Ohio for 48 hours.

I'm not sure what the charge for checking a second suitcase is intended to accomplish, if it's not to make the planes lighter. Sure, the airlines will generate some additional income, until passengers learn to stuff everything into one suitcase. Then they'll come up with more creative ways to generate income.

In fact, some airlines now charge to check your first suitcase, now matter how much it weighs. What's next? Charging to use the restroom in flight or breathe pressurized cabin oxygen?

Some airlines are apparently trying to save a few bucks by flying more slowly. I read that one airline expected to save $42 million in one year by extending each flight by two or three minutes.

Let me get this straight. First you make me cram everything I need into one suitcase (and still keep it under 50 pounds) while you turn around and add extra weight to the plane? And now you're going to fly more slowly (as if being suspended magically in the atmosphere for hours isn't nerve-wracking enough already)?

How about a compromise?

I'll agree to pay an extra $25 for a suitcase filled with shoes so that you don't need to add ballast to the plane. I'll be patient and wait three more minutes to get to my destination. In exchange, you'll let me collect tips as I undress in the security line.

If I have to remove half of my clothing just to get to my gate I might as well get something in return.

With a long enough wait going through security, I could make enough money to pay for that extra suitcase filled with magazines.

19
The Insanity of Motherhood

I was talking with a friend recently about parenting or, more specifically, how mothers throughout history have managed to maintain their sanity while raising children to become adults who don't call their co-workers "Poopy Head."

We were at a picnic and my friend's two-year-old had just warned me with a smile that he was going to bite me while her three-year-old was determined to shake the table until everyone's plates were either in their laps or on the ground. She desperately tried to maintain her composure while reprimanding them, but I could see it in her eyes: she wanted to throw them both in the trunk of the car until the party was over.

Someone suggested that if she ignored her kids they'd stop acting up. While that might be true in theory, any mother knows that it's impossible to ignore a child banging a spoon on a glass table, and not just because you're worried that someone will get hurt. It's the judgmental 'tsk-tsking' from everyone watching that motivates a mother to yank little Jimmy by the arm and hiss through clenched teeth, "If I have to tell you one more time..."

"You know," I said, catching my glass of lemonade as it was about to tip over, "I was shopping yesterday and this woman came up the greeting card aisle with three kids who were clearly driving her crazy. I know because she told them that if they didn't cut it out she was going to take off her flip flop and beat them with it."

The kids, I explained, had found the section with cards that played music. While they were opening card after card and dancing to snippets of disco songs, their mother was calling down threats upon their heads that involved everything from banishment to their rooms to getting "it" (something harsher than a beating with a flip flop, I assumed).

As a shopper, I wasn't really disturbed by the kids. Just minutes before, I had been opening those same cards and giggling. If they were that amusing to an adult, imagine how tempting they were to a trio of eight and nine-year-olds.

I was more bothered by their mother's threats of bodily harm - until I remembered that when my own daughter was young it seemed as if her goal in life was to slowly drive me insane, mostly by asking the question "What is that?" two hundred times an hour. There were moments when I wondered if either one of us would make it through her childhood alive.

I told my friend that I understood how a steady stream of innocent irritations could build up until a mother is forced to the brink of insanity, where whacking her children with a rubber sandal actually begins to sound like a good idea.

That's when I saw something in her eyes, a glimmer of hope that she wasn't the only mother who had considered boxing up her children and shipping them to Siberia.

Almost every mother alive would tell you that it's a gift to be able to raise children who go on to become productive members of society, people who can change the world. But it's not easy to spend every waking moment in the company of humans who eat their own boogers and who can pluck a cat bald in less than three minutes.

Most mothers won't even admit that it's a blow to the ego to know they can control an entire boardroom of executives but can't make a four-year-old put on clean underwear. They need to know they're not alone.

And so, to my friend and the other mothers of small children: If all you did today was read *Goodnight Moon* forty-two times and keep your kids from flushing the goldfish down the toilet, you did a great job.

Even if your kids still call each other "Poopy Head."

20
The Trouble with Technology

I recently got a glimpse of the "House of Tomorrow" on a TV show about home design and technology. While Judy Jetson's kitchen may seem like the stuff of science fiction, according to people who know about these things, it'll be here before you know it.

Introducing the home that virtually runs itself.

Walk in the front door, and the house greets you by name and initiates a welcome program, complete with pre-set lighting and temperature controls. In the kitchen, built-in computer technology allows you to input a list of ingredients and the kitchen will supply a recipe, displayed right onto your kitchen counter. Forget those sticky recipe cards. When you're done, just turn the counter off. The microwave comes with a barcode reader; scan the popcorn bag and your kernels are popped per Orville's instructions.

Everything operates either automatically or on voice command, and it's all designed to make your life easier. There's even a refrigerator that will call you when someone has left the fridge door open.

If the fridge is so high tech, why doesn't it just close the door itself?

It's bad enough that parents can't get a night out without the kids calling a hundred times to complain that someone is watching MTV without permission, or that someone is breathing someone else's air and had better stop before someone gets it. Now the refrigerator calls with problems, too?

Let's say I'm out to dinner. I'm relaxing, enjoying time with my husband and friends, when all of the sudden my cell phone rings.

"Good evening, this is your refrigerator. I'm calling to inform you that my door is open."

I'm not sure that's very convenient. At the risk of stating the obvious, I can't close the door until I get home. Now I'm going to be worrying throughout dinner if my overpriced half-gallon of all natural, organic ice cream is melting into a pool on the kitchen floor or if the cat has crawled in the fridge for a feline buffet of leftover chicken.

I'd rather be ignorant and deal with the problem when I get home. By then, if I'm lucky, the dog will have licked up the ice cream and it won't matter that the cat ate the leftovers. Dinner will already be thawed for tomorrow.

I'm not sure how to define this new personal relationship with my machines. Apparently my car can now send me an email when its oil is low or the battery is about to die. If we're going to be so chummy, why only email me when there's a problem? Why not drop me a line now and then, just to say hello?

Technology is supposed to make our lives easier, but there are times when it's faster to do things the old-fashioned way. Anyone who has used an automatic paper towel dispenser in a public restroom knows what I'm talking about. You can wave your wet hands repeatedly in front of the little red light until it spits out a piece of towel too small to dry a gerbil, but by the time you've accumulated enough toweling, your hands are already dry from all of the waving - although your sleeves are soaked from the dripping water.

Remember the good old days, when it took less time to crank out paper towels than it takes to jump around in front of the automatic sink trying to get the water to turn on?

Don't get me wrong. I'm especially grateful for technology like email, text messaging and cell phones that enable me to keep in touch with friends and family around the globe.

But if I have to chat up my machines as well, maybe someone could program my refrigerator to call my car when we're out of milk so the car can print out a shopping list when I get to the grocery store. That way, I won't have to stand in the produce aisle trying to remember why I'm there.

That, my friend, would be technology designed to make my life easier.

21

Twilight in Dog Years

The sun had been missing for the last eight October days when suddenly, in the late afternoon, the clouds part to reveal a brilliantly blue sky.

Knowing this could be the last sunshine we see for weeks, I throw on sneakers and a sweatshirt, grab the leash and call, "Natasha? Want to go for a walk?"

Despite the frosty wind, the sun shines warmly as we cross the street, being sure to say hello to The Man in the Tweed Jacket as he sits on his porch smoking a cigar.

Natasha knows this block well. While I walk at a slow, steady pace she bounds ahead, stopping to sniff a telephone pole, then falling behind as I pass her, bounding ahead of me again to repeat the scene.

On the next block, a group of kids are playing football in front of the elementary school, and Natasha's ears perk up as she trots ahead of me. She's familiar with the school, having spent many afternoons on the front lawn waiting for the bell to ring, releasing Cassie from her educational prison.

A lone girl with long blond hair spots us and, making a beeline for Natasha, hops off of her bicycle while asking, "Can I pet your dog?" She plops down cross-legged on the sidewalk and reaches for Natasha, who rewards her with a lick on the face.

"How old is your dog?" the girl asks as she runs her hands over Natasha's back.

I have to stop and think about it.

"Thirteen," I reply, slightly surprising myself with the answer.

"Is she going to die soon?" the girl asks, looking up at me with round, blue eyes while her hands are buried deep in Natasha's fur.

"I hope not." I pause, and my voices catches a bit as I add, "Although thirteen is pretty old for a dog."

"How come dogs live shorter lives than children?"

"Well, they say that a dog ages seven years for every human year they're alive. If that's true then Natasha is really..." I stop to count, surprising myself once again. "Ninety one."

"That's pretty old," the girl agrees. "Does she ever get tired?"

Natasha pulls away from the girl and strains on the leash as she catches a scent in the next yard.

"Sometimes she gets tired," I tell the girl as I start to walk away. "But you gave her a chance for a nice rest. Thank you!"

We continue to the building on the corner, where physically and mentally challenged adults live in an assisted care home. As we turn, I see a familiar scene: A handful of residents pacing up and down the sidewalk in front of the door, some talking to each other, some talking to themselves, most of them smoking, all of them smiling as we pass.

I recognize The Bead Man and stop.

His face lights up. "Oh, let me pet the puppy," he says in his gravely voice, holding his cigarette away as he reaches down for Natasha, who has crawled under his walker. The man's face is half hidden by a floppy fishing hat, and his strands of gold Mardi Gras beads sparkle in contrast with his old gray sweatshirt.

"You're a good puppy, aren't you?" He laughs as Natasha licks his shaking hand. She backs out from under the metal crutch and pulls on the leash to continue our walk.

"Have a nice night," I smile and wave over my shoulder.

"Have a nice night," he echoes, waving until we reach the next corner. "Come back again!"

We turn and for the next two blocks repeat the dance, albeit a bit more slowly.

Bound, sniff, bound, sniff.

We're alone for the rest of our walk.

We round the last corner and are almost back to our neighborhood. I can smell the Tweed Man's cigar as we prepare to cross onto our street. Natasha is no longer stopping to sniff every fence post and her pace has slowed considerably. She's panting and her eyes are focused down the block toward our house, where she knows a biscuit and fresh water wait.

The sun, so brilliant just a half hour ago, has already settled into twilight and I know that soon it will set behind the houses as darkness falls.

22
Walking Detail

I went for a walk today. Not generally a noteworthy event, I know. But on the list of things I like to do, exercise ranks just below changing the litter box and just above dusting.

But walking has been on my mind. I recently read a book by travel writer Bill Bryson, in which he chastises Americans for driving half a mile to go to the store. Apparently in England, people walk miles just to buy milk. And these people actually *like* to walk, not just for the exercise but because they get something out of it mentally or spiritually.

Walking to the store when you can drive seems a bit silly to me. Surely all of that physical exertion has to be bad for your heart.

But this morning, as my fingers hurt from typing, my back hurt from sitting and my brain hurt from thinking, I looked out the window and saw the sun shining and, on a whim, decided to walk to the store to get a newspaper.

I suppose if a whole nation can do it, how dangerous can it be?

I was on a tight writing deadline, but figured I could get the walk over with quickly and get right back to work. I found some sneakers, locked the door behind me and headed down the street, a woman walking with a purpose.

I made a beeline for the grocery store, grabbed a newspaper and was headed home with my mission accomplished when I noticed something I'd missed before: There aren't sidewalks on both sides of the road. On my way to the store, I had either crossed the street or walked in the busy road without really making a conscious decision to do either.

Puzzled, I crossed the street in front of my favorite house. When had they put in this new fence, added the shrubbery and painted the shutters? Funny. I missed all of that work being done, even though I drive by every day.

I stopped at the corner where my daughter had been involved in a minor car accident months before. As I stood there, a funeral motorcade drove past. I realized how fortunate I was that my biggest concern was whether or not I'd meet a column deadline.

As I turned onto my street, I spied a small feather lying in the grass and picked it up. Fascinating, how one little grey feather is mixed with some light brown and red feathers, and before you know it, a chickadee is clothed in splendor and ready for flight.

If God takes care of the birds with such an eye for detail, I suppose He's got my problems under control.

I continued toward home, twirling the feather in one hand and swinging my newspaper in the other, realizing that I had actually enjoyed my walk. Clearly my heart was not in danger of exploding and now my mind was safe as well.

I felt so good, I went home and dusted the furniture.

23

Writing Is a Dangerous Job

If I had a dollar for every time someone told me they wished they had my job, I wouldn't have to do this job anymore. I could fly to the tropics and spend the rest of my life lying on a beach, drinking piña coladas and reading mystery novels.

I don't know what everyone finds so glamorous about what I do. I spend all day in my pajamas. I do shower, but rarely put on makeup or do my hair. I go for days at a time without seeing another human except my husband, and depending upon what kind of day he's had, he may not even count.

Trust me, there's nothing glamorous going on around here.

I think people are drawn to the perceived freedom that comes with my job. They think I lie around all day doing nothing and get paid for it. Ha! Wouldn't that be nice?

The reality is that writing is a dangerous job.

For example, I once almost electrocuted myself while writing a column. I was sitting on a metal folding chair at my desk (another benefit of working at home: high class office furniture) and the chair was missing the rubber tip on one of its legs. The power cord to my printer was under that leg and as I fidgeted around in the chair the metal leg sliced through the cord and shorted out the printer.

There was a flash of light and a puff of smoke, and I was left with a large scorch mark on the hardwood floor. I'm convinced that if I hadn't been wearing rubber-soled slippers, I would have been toast.

Another hazard is weight gain. Not only do I sit on my behind all day, when I'm stumped for a story idea, I eat. If there's nothing good to eat, I bake. Even now, I'm itching to whip up a batch of chocolate chip biscotti, which I will undoubtedly eat in its entirety tomorrow while I stare at the computer screen trying to come up with another story idea.

Trust me; you can try and curb your cravings with rice cakes, but in the end only chocolate will get the creative juices flowing.

Let's not forget what happens mentally when you spend all day with no one to talk to but a cat, two dogs and six chickens. It starts out innocently enough, giving your dog a command to turn down the radio or asking the cat what he wants for breakfast. But when you find yourself in the grocery store asking the eggs if they know who their mommy is, you've reached the point of no return.

Everyone asks me where I get my story ideas. If there's one question that'll send a writer over the edge, it's that one.

We all live in constant fear that today's idea will be our last, that tomorrow the well will run dry and we'll be sitting there with a deadline looming and wind whistling through our ears. And as anyone who suffers from panic attacks can tell you, something *potentially* happening is the same as it *actually* happening, so the resulting anxiety from the possibility of writer's block can really wreak havoc on your nerves.

Which, of course, makes you want to eat. Or bake.

And that's just the beginning. We haven't even gotten to carpal tunnel syndrome, back and neck problems caused by hours spent hunched over the keyboard, fingers slammed in filing cabinet drawers, or the possibility of an IRS audit because you claimed a case of White Zinfandel as an office expense.

Of course, there are benefits to writing. I have a staff made up of dogs, a cat and chickens, which makes me the smartest person in my office and also the highest paid.

How's that for a confidence boost?

Yes, I do set my own hours, which means that if I'm feeling creative in the morning, I work in the morning. If I come up with a brilliant idea at midnight, I write at midnight.

My doctor told me - and this is the God's honest truth - that it's healthy to take a nap every day, so I should go ahead and snooze for a half hour every afternoon.

Probably couldn't do that at a real job, even with a doctor's note.

As for running out of ideas? There's always something happening that's worth writing about. And when I'm truly stumped, Bandit can always take over.

It's a tough job, but somebody's got to do it.

24

Smooth Talker

Standing in line at the grocery store, I watched Spencer, the checkout boy, as he talked a blue streak to the middle-aged mom ahead of me in line, exuding youthful energy as he scanned broccoli and toilet paper, bantering with her young boy about how great it is to be sick because you get to miss school and watch cartoons all day.

When it was my turn in line, Spencer greeted me with his usual "How's it going? Did you find everything you were looking for?" and then suddenly said, "You have amazing eyes. What color are they? Blue? Green?"

"I don't know," I replied, a bit startled. "It kind of depends on what color I'm wearing, I guess."

"You don't know? Well, you're wearing grey, so today they're blue."

He flashed his surfer smile and shook his shaggy bangs out of his eyes as he stuffed my chicken and cat food into a bag.

The grey he was referring to could have been the old grey hooded sweatshirt I was wearing, or the dark circles underneath my eyes that come from a lack of sun or sleep, or maybe the stray grey hair that was poking out of my messy ponytail. Either way, it was clearly not a come on; I have leftovers in my refrigerator older than this kid. It's just his natural personality, his ease with himself and with others, his ability to simply make conversation, unable to not converse.

I'd seen Spencer once before, stood in line while he carried on a lengthy conversation with a little girl about her favorite pop star, oblivious to the chaos in the store, focusing only on the girl as he methodically scanned her mother's groceries.

I told him then that he was good with kids and asked if he had younger brothers or sisters. He said he had sisters.

"Older sisters?" I had asked then. "Are you the baby of the family?"

"How did you know," he'd laughed.

I just shook my head.

"You're quite the talker, Spencer," I told him today as I swiped my discount card.

He shook his bangs again and grinned. "They tell me I'm a *smooth* talker."

"That smooth talking could serve you well in life, depending on what you want to do," I replied. I was thinking law or business. This kid could sell ice cubes to

Eskimos. "What are you, in high school? Just graduating?"

He smiled and nodded. "I'm going to be a drifter. I decided that way back in second grade."

"Well, you're certainly cut out for that kind of life, kiddo," I said as I grabbed my bags. "I can see you now, smooth talking your way across the country, then living the surfer life."

"Really?" he asked, almost serious. "That's so cool. Have a great day!"

As I walked to my car, I tried to remember what it felt like to be that age, unencumbered with the burdens of mortgage payments and work deadlines and car repair bills; young enough to still dream, to be so exuberant about life that you couldn't help but share that energy with everyone you came in contact with.

Then I remembered my own frustrations that day, my sadness at the news that my cat was dying, my exhaustion at life in general, and realized that sometimes all you need to brighten your day is a dose of youthful innocence and a glimpse at the promise of all life has to offer.

It's been a few years since that interaction with Spencer. I imagine he's drifted his way across the country, flashing his smile and charming middle-aged mothers on his journey to live the surfer life on the Pacific coast. His career choice may not change the national economy or bring about world peace, but his carefree attitude can be a lesson to us all: If you have to interact with people you can choose to do it with a smile and make them feel special in the process.

25

The Story of Christmas
by Bandit

Guess what! It is almost Christmas time and pretty soon we will have parties and Santa will come and leave lots of presents. Do you know why?

Once upon a time a man named Joseph and his wife Mary were traveling across the country to a family reunion. On the way, they stopped at a hotel. Mary wasn't feeling so good. I guess riding on a donkey for eleven hundred miles can make you feel pretty barfy.

It was not a hotel like the one me and Mommy stayed at when we went on our adventure to Washington, D.C. That was a nice hotel with very nice people.

Joseph and Mary stopped at a not nice hotel with not nice people. When they went inside, the check-in guy said, "Too bad, buster. You don't have a reservation and we don't have any rooms."

Joseph said to the check-in guy, "Can't you see my wife Mary has a really bad belly ache from riding on a donkey for eleventeen hundred miles? Don't you have *any* place we can sleep?"

The check-in guy, who it turns out wasn't so mean after all, said, "Gee, Mister. I am very sorry your wife feels barfy. But I really don't have any rooms. I guess you could stay out in the barn."

The barn is where the people who stayed at the hotel kept their camels and donkeys and horses overnight. There were also some cows and chickens and sheep and elephants and at least one giraffe and some Border Collies to keep everyone in line.

There may have even been a unicorn, but Scout told me that and I think he was fibbing.

So Joseph and Mary went to the barn and they unloaded their donkey-mobile. It was pretty stinky in the barn, but Mary didn't care because she was really tired. So she and Joseph made an itchy bed of hay and went to sleep.

Here is a big secret: Mary had a bad belly ache because she was waiting for a baby to get delivered!

Most people think that the stork delivers babies. But that is not true. The UPS man delivers them. I would not lie about that.

During the night, the UPS man came to the hotel to deliver the baby for Mary and Joseph. And not just any baby. It was Jesus, God's son! The UPS man didn't want to wake everyone up, so he left the baby in the manger.

Just in case you didn't know, a manger is what the animals eat out of. So in the morning, the animals woke up and, *Ta Da!* There was God asleep in their breakfast!

What would you do if you went to eat breakfast and God was sleeping on your plate? I think that would be a very big surprise.

But Mary and Joseph were not surprised. In fact, they were super happy! So they had a big birthday party to welcome Jesus to the world. God's angels invited everyone, including some sheep herders and some kings.

Santa Claus got the invitation on Facebook and thought it would be nice to bring Jesus some birthday presents. So Santa and the elves loaded the sleigh and went to the party. They brought games and a drum and some roller skates and a squeaky ball, because babies like toys that squeak. Just like Border Collies! It was a big, giant party.

And that is why we have parties at Christmas and why we get presents from Santa.

And just so you know, Jesus was never on Santa's naughty list. Unlike some dogs I know.

Merry Christmas!

Your pal,
BANDIT!

26

The Perfect Gift

Ah, Christmas, that wonderful time of year when brightly-wrapped gifts under the twinkling tree contain treasures untold - like a reindeer sweater with a light-up nose, or a gift certificate to a store whose clothes you haven't fit into since junior high.

"I saw this and immediately thought of you," the gift-giver beams, while you're wondering what it was you've said or done to make them think membership in the Vegetable-of-the-Month Club would be high on your holiday wish list.

I've tried to make gift giving easier on my family by giving them specific ideas. Last year, for example, I told my husband that I really wanted a gift certificate to the office supply store.

"I'm not giving you that," he said.

I explained that it was a perfect present considering my office supply addiction, but he wasn't going for it.

"It's too impersonal."

"OK, then, why don't you get me a plastic file crate, and fill it with stuff. I could use some manila folders, paper clips and staples, and I really need a new highlighter, and some toner for my printer..."

"I'm not giving you office supplies for Christmas," he said, and that was his final answer.

Fortunately, he passed my gift certificate request along to his brother. In January, when I was out of both printer toner and money, I was thankful someone had finally listened to me.

The good thing about my mother is that she really wants to give gifts you'll like. If you give her an idea, she'll find a creative way to make your wish come true in a way that also feeds her own addiction to discount, dollar and surplus stores.

Last year, I told her I really wanted family pictures.

My mother has suitcases and boxes under her bed filled with photos of my sister and me as kids, and of family and events long forgotten.

"That's all?" she said. "Old pictures?"

I could sense her disappointment. That idea wouldn't leave much room for creativity on her next shopping spree at the stuff-mart.

"Yes," I assured her. "I want pictures."

She shrugged her shoulders and said, "OK. If that's what really you want."

On Christmas Eve, she handed me two wooden boxes decorated with snowmen (proving that the discount store has something for even the most difficult person on your gift list). The boxes were filled with family photos.

"Awesome!" I said, pulling out picture after picture and passing them around the room. "Look at this. When I was seven or eight, I dressed up like Carol Burnett for Halloween. Look at how young Grandpa looks in this picture. Wow, is this you, Mom?"

There were photos of aunts and uncles, my grandparents and other relatives whose faces mirrored our own. "Look at the family resemblance!" we cried.

The annual school pictures of me and my sister, chronicling our descent from kindergarten adorable to junior high nerd, made us giggle, and we teased each other ("You look exactly the same!") while my mother repeatedly assured us that we were both beautiful.

I put the lid on the last box.

"Thanks, Mom," I said. "This was the perfect gift."

And I meant it.

I suppose that it's probably time to make a wish list for this Christmas, but there isn't really anything I need. I already have more stuff than I know what to do with and I'm actually all set for office supplies.

Besides, Christmas is about more than what Santa leaves under the fir tree. It's remembering the perfect gift that arrived more than 2,000 years ago, wrapped in swaddling clothes and tucked into a manger under a starry Bethlehem sky.

Thirty-three years later, it was given again, wrapped this time in a crown of thorns and nailed on a wooden cross at Calvary.

When it comes to presents, everything else pretty much pales in comparison.

27

The Unsung Celebrity

He looked like just another fresh-faced, Midwestern college student heading back to classes after spring break. Tall and handsome, dressed in jeans, a hooded sweatshirt and baseball cap, he was surrounded by what could only be his family, gathered together to send him back into the big world.

I was returning home to Rochester, NY after spending three days in Dayton, OH for the Erma Bombeck Humor Writer's Conference, where we'd been encouraged to see the humor in the mundane, the laughter in our surroundings and the comedy in our pain.

Maybe that's why I noticed the young man. A woman I assumed was his mother was wrapped tightly around his waist, reluctant to say goodbye, a gesture I was all too familiar with whenever I used to send my daughter back to college, an entire hour from home.

I was with two other women from the conference, chatting and laughing, and the young man ended up behind us in the security line. I leaned across our group and tapped him on the arm. "Where are you going that your family is going to miss you so much?" I asked with a smile.

"The DMZ in South Korea," he responded politely.

It took a minute for that to sink in. The DMZ is the Demilitarized Zone. He wasn't a student. He was a soldier.

Suddenly this wasn't so funny. I looked beyond him, and noticed that his family was still gathered beyond the security ropes, his mother teary-eyed and wringing her hands, not daring to take her eyes off her son for even a moment lest she lose him forever in the crowd.

I leaned back to the young man. "What's your name?"

"Kyle," he replied.

"I'm going to pray for you, Kyle," I promised, and turned around, not sure what else to say.

We were directed through different security lines, and Kyle was through the checkpoint before me. As I met up with my friends and we headed to the coffee shop before going our separate ways, I saw Kyle off to one side putting his belongings back into his carry-on. I wanted to stop and talk to him, but I didn't know what to say. I wanted to run back and tell his family that he would be OK, but I didn't know if that was true.

So I said nothing, and headed for the coffee shop, where I found a group of reality TV celebrities who had been in town for a charity event. Chatter and laughter poured out into the terminal, and fans were getting autographs and taking pictures. I had my picture taken just for kicks.

As I put my camera back into my bag, I looked down the terminal and noticed Kyle walking by himself to his gate. In an instant, the contrast between the pseudo-celebs and Kyle became all too clear.

I was standing with a group of people who were admired simply because they'd been on television, enduring a month on some tropical island, eating coconuts and rice, and battling each other for a cash prize and the chance of product endorsements. They were surrounded by fans who wanted to shower them with attention.

And here was Kyle, headed out to endure a real bout with survival. Real enemies, real sacrifice, real danger. And no one noticed him.

I know almost nothing about Kyle. Surely, he is someone's son. Quite possibly, he is someone's brother. Very likely, he is some young woman's Prince Charming.

But I know now what I want to say to you, Kyle.

You are the foundation upon which this country is built, young men and women willing to leave behind safety, security and family so that I may remain at home and enjoy the fruits of freedom, even if that includes watching mindless television and writing columns just for laughs.

You are more than any television survivor, more middle-American than any Average Joe. You, Kyle, are my hero.

I missed my chance. You are the real celebrity, and I should have had my picture taken with you.

28

What the Dog Said

The dog came near and looked me in the eye. Then he licked my face and sat in my lap.

"Nice to meet you," said the dog. "I think we could be friends."

"I think we already are," I replied. So I took him home.

"Let's play!" said the dog.

"Let's play!" I replied. So we chased bubbles and we chased the wind and we chased the butterflies that fluttered by.

"I'm so happy," said the dog.

"You are happiness itself," I replied. So we touched foreheads and kissed each other on the nose and let the sun shine on our faces.

Time passed and the dog said many things.
"We are a good family."
"Isn't birdsong the best song of all?"
"We are never lonely when we're together."
"I love you."

"I'm afraid," said the dog one day, as thunder clouds rolled overhead.
"I will always be here to protect you," I replied. So the dog crawled into the bed and together we weathered the storm.
"Are you ever afraid?" asked the dog.
"Not when I am with you," I replied.

Time passed and the dog said many things.
"Let's always take care of each other."
"Doesn't sunshine make your eyes happy?"
"Squirrels are such silly creatures."
"I love you."

"Let's see how high I can jump!" said the dog one day.
"Yes, let's!" I replied. And the dog jumped and the dog fell and the dog was hurt. The dog cried and I cried while the lady in the white coat fixed the dog's leg.
"You're sad," said the dog a few days later.
"I feel guilty because you broke your leg," I replied.
"It wasn't your fault," said the dog. "But if you need it, I forgive you." So I cried and took care of the dog every moment of every day until his leg healed.
"Let's play!" said the dog, on the day his leg was free.
"Let's play!" I replied. "But no jumping today."

Time passed and the dog said many things.
"Rainy days were made for taking naps."
"Don't you love things that squeak?"
"Paws can never be too muddy!"
"I love you."

"I don't feel well," said the dog one day.
"I'll help you feel better," I replied. So we went to see the lady in the white coat. She touched the dog with her warm hands and gave us a potion and blessed the dog with kind words.
"I feel better!" said the dog the next day.
"I'm so glad," I replied. So we hugged and we kissed and we played in the sunshine.

Time passed and the dog said many things.
"Butterflies are beautiful."
"Isn't snow the best thing in the world?"
"My tummy hurts a little bit."
"I love you."

"I don't feel well," said the dog one day.
"I'll help you feel better," I replied. So we went to see the lady in the white coat again.
"I think we need to take a picture," she said, so we went to the hospital to see a man in a white coat. He held up the picture and shook his head.
"I don't like it here," said the dog.
"I don't like it either," I replied. "But I promise I won't leave you."
The man in the white coat talked for a long time about what he would do to the dog. He used big words

and touched the dog with cold hands and pronounced the verdict in a dark voice.

"I'm scared and I want to go home," said the dog.

"I'm scared, too," I replied. "I will take you home." So we went home. The next day we went to see the lady in the white coat again. She touched the dog with her warm hands and mixed a new potion and blessed the dog with kind words.

"I feel better!" said the dog the next day.

"I'm so glad," I replied.

Time passed and the dog said many things.
"Let's chase the wind!"
"Is it possible to run out of kisses?"
"Thank you for never leaving me."
"I love you."

"Let's play!" said the dog every day.

"Let's play!" I replied every day. So we chased bubbles and we chased each other and we chased the sun, every day.

Time passed and the dog said many things.
"Sometimes food doesn't taste good."
"Why does my tummy hurt?"
"Please don't leave me."
"I love you."

"Can you make me feel better?" said the dog one day.

"I will try," I replied. So we went to see the lady in the white coat again. She touched the dog with warm hands and mixed more new potions and blessed the dog with more kind words.

"I like the lady in the white coat," said the dog. "She smells like happiness."

"I hope her happiness will help you feel better," I replied. And it did.

Time passed and the dog said many things.
"Friends are a great gift."
"Don't you love to chase bubbles?"
"I'm a little tired."
"I love you."

"You play and I'll watch," said the dog one day.

"It's no fun without you," I replied. But I blew bubbles anyway and I chased the wind while the dog watched and laughed.

"You look sad," said the dog.

"I'm sad because you don't feel well," I replied. So the dog got up and chased one bubble.

Sometimes the dog played. Sometimes the dog watched. One day the dog came near and looked me in the eye. Then he licked my face and sat in my lap.

"I'm sick," said the dog.

"Yes, you are sick," I replied. And we both knew I could not make him feel better.

Time passed and the dog said few things.

"I'm tired," said the dog one day.

"I'll rest here with you," I replied. And we sat together in the sun and watched the bubbles float and the butterflies flutter by.

"You're crying," said the dog. "Are you in pain?"

"It's alright," I replied. "It is only my heart breaking." And I buried my face in the dog's neck as my tears soaked his fur.

"I don't want to hurt you," said the dog.

"You're not hurting me," I replied. "My heart is breaking to make room so I can carry your pain."

"I would do anything for you," said the dog.

"And I would do anything for you," I replied.

"My tummy hurts a lot," said the dog some days later.

"I think maybe it is time for me to carry your pain," I replied.

"I think so, too," said the dog.

I could not reply.

We sat on the floor in the office of the lady with the white coat. The dog laid his head on my lap.

"You know I don't ever want to leave you," said the dog.

"And I don't ever want you to go," I replied.

"But I'm so very tired and so very sick," said the dog.

"Then I will help you find rest," I replied.

"Thank you," said the dog. Then he closed his eyes and found peace.

Time passed. For a long while, no bubbles floated and the sun did not shine. Then one day a butterfly fluttered by.

"The dog says he loves you," said the butterfly.

"I can hear him!" I cried.

"The dog says that every time you feel your heart beat, that is his heart beating with you," said the butterfly.

"I can feel him!" I cried.

"The dog says that it is time for you to forgive yourself," said the butterfly.

And I cried.

Thanks

The columns in this book would not have been possible without the support of friends and family too numerous to count. A few who deserve special mention:

Darling husband David, who works a real job so I can play with words (and dogs) all day. I love you for that and so much more.

My creative, talented and very funny daughter Cassie, who really ought to write a book herself someday.

My parents, Judy Keltz and Jim Keltz, who love me no matter how many stupid things I've done.

Jacqueline Yockey, my sister and frequent partner in crime.

Flow Hick and Brigitte Lefebvre, dear friends and creative cheerleaders of the highest order.

The entire staff at Penfield Veterinary Hospital.

Dozens of editors and publishers who have supported me and published my columns over the years, but especially John Lanier, Executive Editor, *Christian Voice Magazine*, and everyone with the Fellowship of Christian Newspapers, the finest editors and publishers a writer could hope to work with.

Bryan Alexis, for his amazing cover design. Many, many thanks for your creativity and generosity!

Mike and Paula Parker, and everyone at WordCrafts Press, not just fabulous publishers but dear, dear friends. Thank you for working with me!

About the Author

Humor columnist and award-winning freelance writer Joanne Brokaw has spent the majority of her writing career covering entertainment, writing feature stories and penning a slice-of-life column for dozens of newspapers, magazines and websites in the U.S. and Canada. Her extensive writing resume includes *American Greetings*, *Beliefnet.com*, *Patheos.com*, *Christian Examiner* newspapers, *Christian Voice Magazine*, *Focus on the Family*, *Pup Culture Magazine* and *Rochester Woman Magazine*. She also assists her Border Collie, Bandit, with his blog and answers his fan mail.

In addition to writing, drinking tea and cultivating her flock of dust bunnies, Joanne spends her days dreaming of things she'd like to do but probably never will - like swimming with dolphins, cleaning the attic and someday overcoming the trauma of elementary school picture day. She lives in Western NY with two dogs, a cat, six chickens and one very patient husband. Learn more at **www.joannebrokaw.com**.

Bandit says about himself, "I'm a dog. I do dog stuff and then I write about it." When he's not blogging, he likes to bark, chew socks and run around like a wild animal. Be his friend at:
www.facebook.com/mynameisbandit.

A portion of the sale of each copy of **What The Dog Said** is donated to Rochester Hope for Pets.

Who is Rochester Hope for Pets?

We are a not-for-profit organization whose mission is to improve the quality of life for Rochester area companion animals by: providing financial awards toward veterinary care to pet owners during times of need; assisting veterinary health professionals with continuing education opportunities; and partnering with other animal-related nonprofits in our region.

Since its founding in December of 2008, Rochester Hope for Pets has made more than 720 awards to pet owners and rescue groups for use toward veterinary care at 32 different hospitals in Monroe and surrounding counties. With your help, we can continue to grow and impact many more community members and their pets. Won't you join us?

To make a gift online, go to:
rochesterhopeforpets.org/donate.php

Rochester Hope for Pets
2816 Monroe Avenue
Rochester, NY 14618
RochesterHopeforPets.org

www.ingramcontent.com/pod-product-compliance
Lightning Source LLC
Chambersburg PA
CBHW071408290426
44108CB00014B/1730